AN ILLUSTRATED TOUR
Color Your Way Through Gilford's History

COURTNEY PARSONS   **KATHY LACROIX**   **HEIDI SMITH**

An Illustrated Tour
Color Your Way Through Gilford's History

Library of Congress Control Number: 2022914021

Paperback ISBN: 979-8-9854340-6-4

Book Cover, Design and Layout: Courtney Parsons

Editor: Jane Stucker

Book Collaborator: Heidi Smith

Give a Salute! provides publishing services to the author(s) specifications and approval. The author retains all responsibilities and rights to the content of this book.

DEDICATION

This coloring book is dedicated to all residents of Gilford and the Lakes Region-past, present, and future. I am indebted to Gilford's Thompson-Ames Historical Society and the Gilford Village Historical District Commission for recognizing that there needed to be a book written detailing the town's history, and to Adair D. Mulligan and the many volunteers who contributed to the writing of "The Gunstock Parish: A History of Gilford, New Hampshire." I simply tried to condense information largely found in her book into this brief booklet. Also, thank you to Heidi Smith for her encouragement and help, to Courtney Parsons for her delightful and whimsical drawings, and to Give a Salute! Publishing Company.

Kathy Lacroix, On behalf of the Thompson-Ames Historical Society

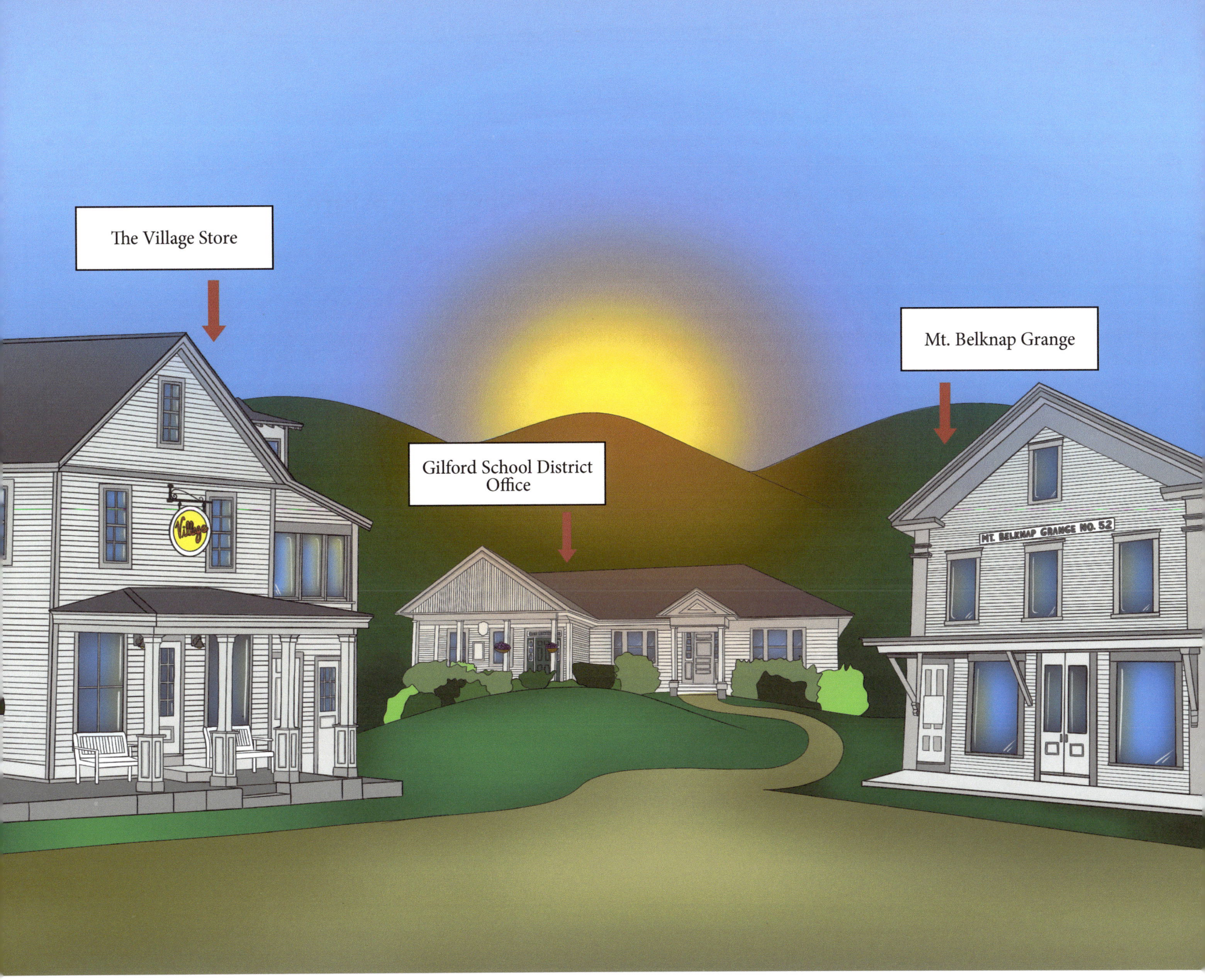

The Village Store

Gilford School District Office

Mt. Belknap Grange

The Recreation Center of New Hampshire

Gilford was originally known as Gilmanton's Upper Parish or the Gunstock Parish. In March of 1776, Samuel F. Gilman paid his grandfather 5 pounds for 40 acres of land, and in 1776 or 1777, he moved to his lot on Gunstock Hill. John Bennett, Jr. purchased his lot on Liberty Hill a month later, and James Ames set up his farm in the Intervale around the same time. The first permanent settlers had arrived.

There are two theories as to the origin of the name "Gunstock," one being that as Greene Chase raised his gun to kill an attacking cougar, the hammer on his musket broke, and he had to use his gun to hit and kill his prey, breaking the gun stock. Another is that a company of hunters, in felling a tree, happened to break the stock of one of their guns. However, the upper part of Gilmanton began to be referred to as Gunstock Parish, and there is now a Gunstock Hill Road and a Gunstock Mountain.

As time went on, Gilford became a prosperous community of farms and industries. It was difficult to travel to the Lower Parish for town meetings, and some resented sending their tax money to benefit a community so far away. On June 16, 1812, Gilford was incorporated as a town. The honor of naming the new town was given to a Revolutionary War hero, Lieutenant Mason, who named it in honor of an important battle that was fought at the Guilford Courthouse in North Carolina in 1781. No one knows if he did not know how to spell the name correctly or if the clerk made the error.

Today, Gilford provides excellent recreational opportunities for residents and visitors. The county-owned four season Gunstock Recreation Area is enjoyed by skiers, hikers, and campers. Ellacoya State Park offers many family-friendly options, an excellent beach, sites for picnics, and a RV campground. Boaters enjoy the waters of Lake Winnipesaukee. There are many hiking trails in Gilford that are free and maintained by volunteers, such as Kimball Castle and the Weeks trails.

Gilford Village Store

The Gilford Village Store opened in 1836, and was owned by Benjamin Jewett 3rd, Albert Chase, and Jeremiah Thing. At one time, there were three stores in the area, but this is the only one that survived a succession of owners and remodeling. It has an 1870s storefront with its centrally-located doors and large panes of glass. And at one time, entertainment was presented upstairs. The local Grange members also held their meetings there before they bought the defunct store across the street.

The Village Store still offers a few basic grocery items and now specializes in deli and bakery products. With its cozy dining area, it is a community gathering area where one may go for a cup of coffee and a breakfast or lunch sandwich. It also provides take-out service.

Fun Fact: During the annual Holiday Candlelight Stroll in December, it offers special cookies to those who are strolling through the Village.

Photo provided by Courtney Parsons

Gilford School District Office

The Gilford School District Office at 2 Belknap Mountain Road was originally built and used as a library. With town appropriations, much volunteer labor and donated land from the Reverend and Mrs. Wilbur Harding, it was built in 1924-1925, for a total cost of under $5000, with an addition in 1983-1984, that cost $131,000.

When the new library opened in 2008, the town needed to research how this building could be used, since the land was donated for the purpose of being used for the library. Learning that it could be used by the school district, it was voted at the 2010 town meeting to lease it to them.

Fun Facts: Besides being quiet and respectful, patrons showed/practiced self-control, as it was not until 1962, that a small area of the library was portioned off, and the first toilet was installed.

Standing on the bridge adjacent to the building, one can see the stonework that was part of the foundation of the first sawmill in town in 1789. The building stands on what was once part of the mill yard where logs were stored until they could be sawed into lumber.

Photo provided by Courtney Parsons

Mt. Belknap Grange No. 52

Colonel John J. Morrill built this Greek Revival building in 1857, for Levi Thompson's store. In 1909, his son sold it to the Grange, and in 1990, the Grange deeded it to the Thompson-Ames Historical Society. It is listed on the National Register of Historical Places as a well-preserved example of a mid-nineteenth century country store with good Greek Revival detailing. Key features include the wide cornerboards that terminate in molded caps and frieze boards. Besides being a store, it also served as the post office.

The Gilford's Thompson-Ames Historical Society renovated the main building to resemble the store as it was originally. Besides having many items that could have been bought in an early store, there are numerous farm tools displayed along one wall, plus a display with early shoes and all the tools needed to make them. There is also a stand that once held incoming mail until the recipient came to town to pick it up.

Where once the open horse stalls were on the left of the store, the Grange members enclosed them and created a kitchen that was put to use for their Grange suppers. The Society has maintained it with its original features, and they have also kept the Grange meeting room above the store.

The open-faced woodshed has been enclosed, and the Society renovated it to resemble a one-room homestead that early settlers might have lived in when they first came to Gilford.

Fun Fact: Penny candy may still be bought in the store, and the penny is deposited and rung up in the old cash register.

Photo provided by Thompson-Ames Historical Society

Gilford Public Library

Gilford lost its first public library in Lakeport when its residents voted to leave Gilford and become part of Laconia. In 1893, the town voted to appropriate $50 to establish a new free public library, and the state furnished $100 worth of books. With 40 books donated by residents and a total of 232 books, the library opened in the northwest parlor of the Deacon Hunter House in the center of the village, with Carrie Hunter Gill as volunteer librarian. In the spring of 1897, the library moved to the first floor of the old town hall. Its growing collection of 1,659 volumes needed more space so it moved upstairs five years later.

From 1907 on, many townspeople thought that a proper library building should be built. With several town appropriations, much volunteer labor, and donated land from the Reverend and Mrs. Wilbur Harding, it was built in 1924-1925, for a total cost of under $5000. The construction of a public library building through private philanthropy was typical in New Hampshire at this time.

As the town grew, it became evident that space was limited and left little in the way for potentially growing the collection and additional offerings. The library that many frequent today was opened on August 18, 2008, and was dedicated to local residents Dick and Betty Persons. They had donated 3 million dollars to start the town/private partnership that enabled the library to be built. Local residents/volunteers moved all the old books from the old library to the new one. Today, many volunteer there every week. With plenty of space for its vast collection of books, it now offers other amenities such as CDs, access to computer terminals, a children's room, a teen's room, and a dedicated meeting room where many programs are offered.

Photo by Courtney Parsons

Fun Fact: As part of Old Home Day, the library hosts a pie and ice cream social under the tent outside. All are welcome.

GILFORD PUBLIC LIBRARY

Old Town Hall

When Gilford became a town in 1812, election for town officials and meetings was held in the Gunstock meetinghouse (no longer in existence). In 1841, the old town hall was built on Potter Hill Road in the village. At first, it had only a large single room. The selectmen, town clerk, and tax collector all worked out of their homes, as the hall was mainly used for public meetings. After records were lost due to house fires, it was decided that business would no longer be done in homes but would move to the town hall. In 1885, a vault was installed to keep records safe. The vault and its installation cost $215.

As the town grew, changes were made to the building, since more positions were created and more staff was needed. As the town had acquired the 1838 Rowe House and the land (then known as the Wilson Farm) so as to build its school, that building was also used for town offices. By the 1980s, the town had outgrown its space, and the new town hall was built in 1988.

Gilford residents value their heritage and prefer to repurpose its old buildings rather than tear them down. In 1990, the Gilford Community Church bought the vacant old hall for one dollar and moved it back onto a new foundation and connected it to the church. It is now called the Wixson Center (in honor of the minister who saw its possibilities to be of use once again), and the preschool program there now serves the community.

Fun Fact: Donors to Gilford's Thompson-Ames Historical Society rescued the door to the vault with "Town of Gilford" in gilt letters, and you may now see it as you enter the lobby of the town hall.

Photo provided by Thompson-Ames Historical Society

Potter Hill Farm

The Potter Farm on Potter Hill is representative of many of the farms in early Gilford. In 1794, Joseph Potter bought his 100-acre homestead from Nathan Hoit, and the farm remained in his family for 150 years, with four generations living there, until 1944. Besides raising cattle and sheep on his farm, he was a shoemaker and cord-wainer (leather worker) and served the town as inspector of leather.

Just as Joseph Potter was both a farmer and a shoemaker, many farmers practiced a craft from their home, such as building a cooper's shop to make barrels in between doing farm chores. Many farmers had apple orchards and took pride in making their apple cider. Others planted and raised flax which could be used to make linseed oil, and its fibers could be woven into cloth. The wool from sheep could be spun into skeins and either be knitted for socks, hats, and mittens or woven into cloth.

The good agricultural land attracted the first settlers, and most of the first farms were multi-purpose farms. By the 1880s, many farmers had large herds of milking cows and sold directly to customers or to factories for butter and cheese. But in 1985, the last dairy herd was sold, and large-scale farming had ceased.

Fun Fact: When Joseph Potter's great-grandson, Fred Potter, sold his home in 1944, he donated some of the early household items and farming implements to Gilford's Thompson-Ames Historical Society. They may be seen at the 1857 Mt. Belknap Grange and at the 1834 Union Meetinghouse, both on Belknap Mountain Road, in the heart of the village.

Photo provided by Thompson-Ames Historical Society

Tannery Hill Covered Bridge

The Tannery Hill Covered Bridge is a single-span 48-foot wooden Town Lattice truss design that was popular in the U.S. in the 1820-1850s, and spans the Gunstock Brook in Gilford. It connects the parking lot of the town hall with Tannery Hill Road leading to the Gilford Historical District. A tannery had once been in operation near the site; hence the name of the road and the bridge. At one time, there was a full-size bridge, but it had been removed in the 1950s.

Local resident Tim Andrews, who was an experienced master builder of covered bridges, volunteered to help and assist the volunteers from the Gilford Rotary Club and townspeople as they constructed the bridge in a local warehouse. It took over 2,000 man hours more than four months and $12,000 in materials. Gilford Rotarians, local merchants, and residents paid for its cost. There are 374 oak trunnels (wooden pegs), and residents could "adopt" a peg for $20 or buy T-shirts or glassware.

The Bridge was presented to the town by the Gilford Rotary Club on October 8th, 1995. Gilford's Kathy Salanitro's team of oxen pulled it across the brook as townspeople watched.

Photos provided by Thompson-Ames Historical Society

Fun Fact: You can enjoy a pleasant walk on the bridge, stop and admire the peaceful view and listen to the tranquil sound of the brook. There is a picnic bench under some shade trees, inviting you to sit and enjoy a lunch.

Weeks Bandstand

In 1975, the Gilford Bicentennial Committee decided to build a bandstand as part of the town's celebration of the Nation's Bicentennial, and at the town meeting, $15,000 was approved for that purpose. It was built on land that the town had bought in 1965, and is at the entrance to the Village Field, with the tennis court to the right and the middle high school playing fields at the left.

In the summer of 1976, contractor Bob Swett built a large plain octagonal-shaped structure that had a small crowning cupola with louvered sides and roof of flared eaves. It was dedicated on August 29, 1976, and named the Weeks Bandstand in honor of one of the town's oldest families.

Fun Fact: The Gilford Community Band, formed in 1978, offers free concerts every other Wednesday. People enjoy bringing a lawn chair or a blanket and listening to the volunteer band, ranging in age from high school freshman to adults.

Photo provided by Heidi Smith

The Meetinghouse

In 1834, the Universalist Society built this church as the Gilford Union Meetinghouse. Benjamin Gilman and Captain Benjamin Weeks constructed it, and it had plaster walls and a choir loft. To pay for the construction costs, they sold the pews. The buyers then owned them, and only their family would sit there. In 1874, the Methodist Episcopals bought the church, and in 1889, added the steeple, stained glass windows and beautiful stained hemlock interior walls.

It stood empty for a number of years until George Ames, a local man who had moved to New Jersey, bought it and donated it to the newly-formed Historical Society as a meeting place to display items depicting the town's early years, especially its farming heritage. He requested that it be named the Thompson-Ames Historical Society in remembrance of his parents.

There are seven main sections along the sides with items depicting early Gilford, winter sports, town, military, farming, one-room schoolhouses, church, and a parlor in a home. The Society hosts some of its meetings there.

Fun Fact: In the town section, one can ring the old-fashioned wall-hung telephone and learn about the party line (where those on the line could tell which call was theirs by the number of rings).

Photo provided by Heidi Smith

Gilford Elementary School

The consolidated Gilford Elementary School opened in the fall of 1940, with 121 students in grades 1-8. On the first floor was an auditorium that could seat 225 and was used for stage productions, entertainment and meetings. It also had one classroom that was used for manual training (shop) classes and one for domestic science (sewing) classes. In 1942, a kitchen was added so students could have a hot lunch for the first time. If an upper level student had finished their work, they could sometimes help the lunch lady with her work. Upstairs there were four classrooms for students in grades 1-8, with two grades in each classroom.

There was steam heat, running water, modern toilets (an improvement over the privies/outhouses), large windows, electric lights to provide plenty of light, and fans that would exhaust the "foul air" from each room up to an outlet in the copper roof of the cupola. Since it was built of brick and concrete, it was much safer than the previous wooden one-room schoolhouses.

The town paid Laconia so that their high school students could go to Laconia High School. By 1948, the school was overcrowded so the 7th and 8th graders also went to Laconia. In 1950, 1956, 1962, and 1991, more additions were added. With the building of the Gilford High and Middle Schools, the elementary school now consists of Kindergarten through Grade 4.

Fun Fact: Imagination Station on the playground may be enjoyed by all children on Saturdays and Sundays and any other time when the school is not in session.

Photo provided by Heidi Smith

Under the Mountain School No. 9

When Gilford was incorporated as a town in 1812, there were 10 district/neighborhood one-room schoolhouses for grades 1-12. Students would walk to the one nearest to their home. Each schoolhouse was maintained by a neighborhood committee that made all the decisions concerning the running of their school, hiring the teacher, setting the curriculum, and the number of days it would be open. There were two terms, usually one in the summer and fall and the second in the winter. The length of the term could vary from one district/neighborhood to another. For example, in 1866, district No. 2 offered 13 students only four weeks of instruction in the summer term, while No. 7 ran for eleven weeks. If a student was needed at home during either term, they would stay home to work.

In 1885, the independent districts were replaced by an elected town-wide three-member school board. It was not until 1919, that the State of New Hampshire enacted a law that required a school year of thirty-six weeks. All districts set up their own September to June calendars, which is what we now have.

The Under the Mountain School No. 9 is an example of what an early one-room school was like. It is now owned privately but can be seen at its original location on Hoyt Road, near the old Weeks Cemetery. It was also known as the Weeks School because many Weeks families had settled in the area and their children went there; however, students from as far away as Saltmarsh Pond Road also attended.

The picture shows a corner of the school room that was taken in 1930. Inside the classroom was a pot-bellied stove that was heated by wood. Notice also the outhouse, with a door for the girls and the boys.

Fun Fact: Imagine if you had been a student in 1812 or 1930. Would you have studied the wide variety of subjects that you do now? The 3 R's were most important; reading, (a)rithmetic, and (w)riting.

Photos provided by Thompson-Ames Historical Society

Pine Grove Cemetery

In the early days, many families established burial grounds on a corner or area of their own land, and some gradually became neighborhood cemeteries. There are fourteen family/neighborhood cemeteries in the Town of Gilford.

There was no burying ground at or near Gilford Village until October 31, 1860, when David Gould sold four acres of his farmland to the town for $25.00. When Albanus Rowe, (grandson of Benjamin Rowe who had settled on his farm adjacent to the cemetery in 1815) died, townspeople realized there was a need for a community-wide cemetery with the promise of perpetual care.

Albanus Rowe died of "consumption," now called tuberculosis, at the age of fifteen, after working in his father Simon's shop for three years. He was the first person buried in the cemetery in the Rowe family plot. Simon planted a row of red pines to hide the grave from his grieving wife's view as she worked in the kitchen.

The granite bank wall and arched gateway were built and given to the town by Fred Weeks, who had grown up on his family farm in Gilford and lived there until he moved away.

Photo provided by Courtney Parsons

Fun Fact: It is interesting to stroll through an old cemetery and read what is on the various gravestones. The Rowe family plot may be found on the left side midway up the slope nearest to the row of trees.

The 1838 Rowe House

In 1815, Benjamin Rowe and his family bought the farm and original home from Jesse Thing who had first settled there in 1810. In 1838, he added on to his farmhouse by building a two-story one with bricks he made in his kiln with clay from the brook that ran through his property.

The Benjamin Rowe House is an excellent example of rural Greek Revival architecture, with its sidelights surrounding the center entrance, granite lintels, 9/6 windows, and American bond brick pattern. Inside are the original floors, fireplaces, mantels, cabinets, five-panel doors, and locally-forged iron Norfolk thumb latches. It is the only known brick farmhouse in New Hampshire with four interior chimneys arranged around a central hallway floor plan. At some point, the original farmhouse was demolished; the present wooden ell was added at a later date.

Photo by Courtney Parsons

In 1908, Benjamin's son Simon died, and the home and seventy acres of farmland were sold to Ernest Sawyer who became a dairy farmer. In 1947, it was passed to his son-in-law Alvah Wilson, who continued the dairy farm. The Wilsons sold the land and buildings to the town in 1969, retaining the right to live there for the remainder of their lives. The Gilford Middle High School was built on what had been pastureland. The house was used as a town hall until the decision was made to build a new town hall, and then the New Hampshire Music Festival used it as headquarters for a few years.

The land was needed for the enlargement of the elementary school, and buildings needed to be demolished. However, Gilford residents do not like to demolish their historical buildings. They prefer to repurpose them, and that is what happened in 1989. At the town meeting, a public/private partnership was reached. A volunteer committee raised funds and renovated the building back to what it originally looked like.

Fun Fact: Gilford's Thompson-Ames Historical Society leases the Rowe House and operates it as a museum. Children are encouraged to hold a couple of butter molds and try to guess their purpose, guess what a butter churn is, crank it, and learn the story concerning glass milk jugs.

ROWE HOUSE

THE HOMESTEAD FARM OF BENJAMIN ROWE ONCE INCLUDED
THE SLOPES OF MT. ROWE AND THE FERTILE FLOODPLAIN NOW
OCCUPIED BY THE MIDDLE HIGH SCHOOL. SEVERAL MULBERRY
TREES DATING FROM HIS 1840 ATTEMPT TO FOUND A LOCAL
SILK INDUSTRY SURVIVE ALONG THE FENCE. SOLIDLY BUILT
OF BRICK MADE ON THE SITE, THE RARE FOUR CHIMNEY CAPE
IS ONE OF ONLY SIX EARLY BRICK CAPES IN ALL OF BELKNAP
COUNTY. THE HISTORIC HOUSE REMAINED IN THE ROWE FAMILY
FOR NEARLY A CENTURY, PASSED TO ALVAH WILSON IN 1947 AND
CAME UNDER THE PROTECTION OF THE TOWN OF GILFORD IN 1969.

Kimball Castle

Benjamin Ames Kimball was so impressed with a castle that he had seen in Germany that he wanted to construct a summer home similar to it in Gilford. He chose the location on Lockes Hill that had a spectacular view of Lake Winnipesaukee and hired Italian stonemasons to build it. The stone was quarried from Concord and locally from the south side of Lockes Hill, with many of its furnishing imported from Europe. At the time construction began in 1894, the medieval style was popular for public buildings, such as armories, but was rare for a home.

Benjamin Ames Kimball's home was in Concord, New Hampshire, where he was a railroad executive who had seen the construction of the Lake Shore Railroad through Gilford and its consolidation with the Boston, Concord, and Montreal Railroad. He became its president in 1895. He had a railroad station built below his home to accommodate his guests and the public. He lived there until his death in 1920, and then it passed to his wife and then to his daughter-in-law, Charlotte Kimball, who spent summers there until her death in 1960.

Charlotte Kimball established a trust for the castle property, stating that it be used for the study and enjoyment of wildlife. In 1981, the Town of Gilford was appointed trustee by the State Attorney General and in 1990, named a stewardship committee to develop a wildlife habitat area with interpretive trails on its 280 acres. However, the Castle and its outbuildings are privately owned and have "No Trespassing" signs surrounding it.

Fun Fact: Lockes Hill hiking trails are free and open to the public. The parking lot and trail head are located off Route 11, heading toward Alton.

Photo provided by Thompson-Ames Historical Society

BNH Pavillion-Meadowbrook

In 1996, this outdoor amphitheater opened and was known as the Meadowbrook Farm Pavilion, with temporary staging, 2,500 temporary seats and room for 2,000 lawn guests who would bring their own chairs/blankets. It underwent many improvements and name changes. In 2013, it partnered with the local bank to become known as the Bank of New Hampshire Pavilion and now has 6,000 seats under a covered pavilion, 540 reserved lawn seats, and room for 2,850 general admissions.

When it first opened, it featured stars such as Johnny Cash and Chubby Checker and the following year in 1997, Ray Charles and Willie Nelson (who has been a favorite, performing there for many years). During the summer and fall, it offers a wide variety of big-name performers, with a second smaller stage that features local talent before the main show begins. It is located at 72 Meadowbrook Lane on land that was once part of Meadowbrook Farm.

Photo provided by Thompson-Ames Historical Society

The land had once been farmed by various owners. The Miller family from Massachusetts owned the land and several cottages on it and named their retreat Meadowbrook. For almost a hundred years, members used it for summer vacations, week-end trips and in general for family events. They were musically inclined; many enjoyed playing a variety of instruments, and they would present concerts in their field. Nowadays, professionals perform on the stage, and we can all enjoy their performances.

Fun Fact: It is said that Charles Miller invented the chewy molasses and peanut candy in his kitchen at home in Boston and named it after his favorite aunt, Mary Jane. He opened a factory in Revere and became a successful candy maker, enabling him to buy his vacation home in Gilford. Nowadays the Mary Jane is made by the Texas candy company Atkinson and is slightly changed. It is now a rounded, bite-sized candy in a wrapper with twisty ends. When you buy a Mary Jane candy, think of the Millers of Meadowbrook. They were the first to hold family concerts in their field.

Beans & Greens Farm

The house and the barn that now are part of the Beans & Greens Farm were most likely built by Ebenezer Smith Jr., in 1831. On the second floor hayloft, the initials JS and the date 1857 are carved into a beam. It is speculated that JS might stand for a son or family member. In 1875, the farm was sold to Frank Rand, and the farm remained in the Rand-Harris family for four generations. In its last days as a farm, registered Hereford cattle were in the barn in the winter, and in the summer they grazed in the pastures across the street where farm produce is now grown. The state moved the barn to its present location when Route 11B was rerouted, and it is now listed on the New Hampshire Register of Historical Places.

Andy and Martina Howe bought the property, and with much work, they repurposed the barn and created the Beans & Greens Farm in 1989. Over the years they made many additions, such as adding greenhouses and a gazebo. Besides selling vegetables, plants and flowers, they added a bakery and deli and a petting barnyard. In 2021, they sold the farm stand to Brian McCauley and Chris Collias.

Due to communities raising property taxes higher and higher, many farmers needed to sell off some of their needed farmland to pay taxes. In 1967, the state passed legislation that enabled protection of land through conservation easements, where the land could remain in private ownership. The right to convert it into house lots or other "development" could be separate from the property; hence lower property taxes. In conjunction with the New Hampshire Land and Forest Society, Gilford became the first community in New Hampshire to do this, voting at town meeting in 1984, to purchase a conservation easement on the land across the road from the barn.

Fun Fact: Fun things at the farm include a Harvest Festival and corn maze in the fall and Family Farm Day in the summer. You can also have your birthday party here or enjoy lunch in the pavilion and meet the barnyard animals. They enjoy making new friends!

Photos provided by Heidi Smith

Old Home Day

Governor Frank Rollins established "New Hampshire Old Home Week" at the 1899 session of the legislature to encourage New Hampshire-born people to return to the town of their birth and celebrate their past. He was also hoping that some of them would buy summer homes in or near their home towns and thus help the economy.

In 1919, Gilford held its first Old Home Day. For many years they were held on a Thursday. Then, as now, activities took place in the field that is now known as the Village Field. The Grange members were quite active in planning the events. In the morning there was usually a baseball game on the field, and there were games and relay races for the children, who found it particularly challenging to climb a greased pole to get a prize on top. At noon, there was a baked bean dinner in the Grange Hall, and plates could also be passed out through the windows overlooking the huge copper sink to those sitting on the lawn in the back of the building, or people would bring their own picnic meal. For the adults, there was an afternoon speaker in the town hall while the children played ball outside. In the evening the Grange would present a show or play and then have a dance.

Nowadays, Old Home Day is held on the Saturday before the week of Labor Day. The day starts with the Gilford Rotary hosting a pancake breakfast at the youth center on the grounds of the Gilford Community Church, followed by a parade at 10:00 (this tradition started around 1931), activities, food, and vendors on the Village Field. There are also activities at the library and at the community church, as well as open houses at the Historical Society's Grange, Meetinghouse and Rowe House. The day ends with a concert at the Village Bandstand followed by spectacular fireworks.

Fun Fact: All activities are free, so come and enjoy!

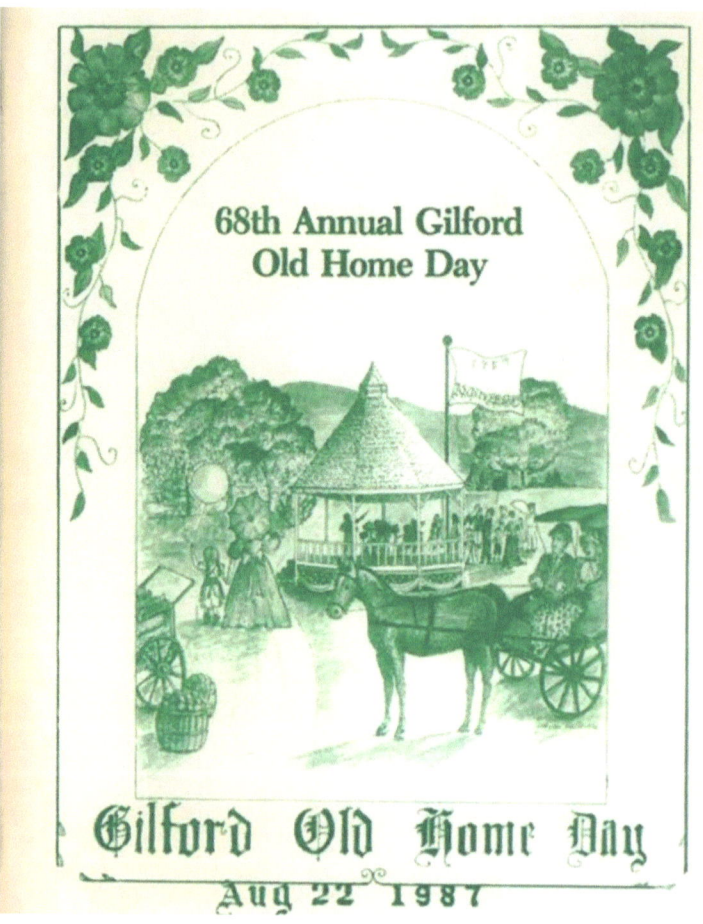

68th Annual Gilford
Old Home Day

Gilford Old Home Day
Aug 22 1987

Photo provided by Thompson-Ames Historical Society

Candlelight Stroll

On the second Saturday in December, from 5:00-7:00 pm, hundreds of candles line the streets, starting at the library on Potter Hill Road and continuing up Belknap Mountain Road. The road is closed to through traffic so people can stroll at their leisure and enjoy the many activities available. Listening to carolers or joining in, enjoying a horse and wagon ride through the village, or the plethora of crafts and activities at the library are all available delights.

You can visit the 1857 Grange and see what an early store might have looked like and enjoy fresh baked cookies in the Grange kitchen before your visit to the early Homestead Room. The Village Store across the street has a smorgasbord of treats to offer or you can continue down the street to the Village Field and make yourself a s'more at the bonfire while visiting Santa. Across the street, the 1834 Meetinghouse is open, a refuge to get warmed up and a chance to join their activities for those who would enjoy doing that.

The Stroll started in 2012, and was the last event that the volunteer Bicentennial Committee planned as the town celebrated its two hundredth birthday. It was so popular that it has continued and is now an official Gilford Town event, run by volunteers and donations.

Fun Fact: It's free so come and enjoy!

Photos provided by Thompson-Ames Historical Society

ABOUT THE AUTHOR

Kathy Lacroix

Kathy Lacroix lived in Gilford for over 50 years in a farmhouse that had been in her husband's family for 200 years. For many years her husband enjoyed being a "part time farmer," and Kathy "the farmer's wife." They tended to the beef cattle and sheep as well as the two piglets who arrived in the spring. In addition, they grew vegetables on their 100-acre farm. She is proud to have lived in a town where its residents value their historical heritage. Old buildings are not torn down, they are restored and adapted, such as an 1857 barn that has a new life, an old town hall that has become a center for a nursery school, old buildings that are now museums, and beautiful old homes.

For 37 years she was an elementary school teacher, 34 of them at Gilford Elementary School. She is on the Board of Gilford's Thompson-Ames Historical Society and enjoys giving tours of the three museums in town. She was part of the Gilford's Bicentennial Committee that originated the Candlelight Stroll.

Courtney Parsons

Courtney Parsons is an illustrator, graphic designer, and a free-lance artist hailing from Laconia, New Hampshire. Above all, she is a nature admirer and an animal lover, both being prominent themes throughout much of her artistic work. Currently, Courtney resides in Northern Virginia, where she works, attends George Mason University, and lives with her fiancé and cat. Courtney has a deep-rooted fondness for the beautiful Lakes Region, and she considers it an honor to be involved in this project with Heidi and the entire team at Give a Salute!.

Heidi Smith

Heidi Smith is a native of New Hampshire's Lakes Region, where she raised her son and still resides. She has spent the majority of her professional career in the local health care setting, celebrating over 37 years.

Her passion for history has led her to many opportunities, one of which is the coloring book series, *Color Your Way USA*. This began after she noticed Courtney Parsons' online drawing of the Colonial Theatre, which is located in Heidi's hometown. Once she saw the illustration, she knew a coloring book series featuring different historical locations throughout the country needed to be created.

Along with Courtney and the staff of Give a Salute!, Heidi and the team put this concept into design, and they are now collaborating with several nonprofits to help raise money for those organizations as a unique way to preserve and interact with history.

We hope you have enjoyed coloring your way through Gilford's history, and you have also learned a little about its past.

To find out how to color your way through your own community's history, we invite you to contact **Give a Salute!** at **giveasalute@gmail.com**. Also, be sure to check out our website at **http://giveasalute.com**.

www.ingramcontent.com/pod-product-compliance
Lightning Source LLC
Chambersburg PA
CBHW040817120626
46551CB00004B/583